IDEAS TO GO

BEHAVIOUR

book is due for return on or before the last date shown below

Ages 6-8

Activities and ideas to develop better behaviour
across the National Curriculum

Dr Helen McGrath

A & C Black • London

CONTENTS

INTRODUCTION

Effective behaviour management has three elements – prevention, 'on-the-spot' management and ongoing behavioural support. Most effort should be put into prevention, to make it less likely that pupils will choose to misbehave. Providing a positive and supportive classroom environment, where pupils are taught specific social and personal skills, will help to ensure that pupils feel safe and accepted at school. This book provides teachers with ideas, activities and strategies to help pupils develop the skills to positively manage their own behaviour and also gives suggestions for dealing with challenging behaviour. The activities can be used to complement classroom work, or as a strategic resource for a particular situation.

ABOUT THIS BOOK

TEACHERS' FILE

The teachers' file offers advice on how to make make the most of this book. It contains ideas for classroom organisation as well as background notes, ICT tips, assessment ideas and suggestions for parental involvement.

QUICK STARTS

This section offers activities, games and ideas that will help teachers to improve pupils' abilities to manage their own behaviour. These activities can be used at any time, with little or no preparation, in any order, and incorporated into the classroom curriculum. Also included in this section is a 'Circle time quick starts' page which gives ideas and simple rules for establishing the use of circle time as part of the classroom routine.

ACTIVITY BANK

The activity bank contains 27 photocopiable activities covering aspects of behaviour management related to the Knowledge, Skills and Understanding outlined in the guidelines for PSHE and Citizenship at Key Stages 1 and 2 (see QCA initial guidance, published in April 2000). The activities can be used in any order and may be modified and adapted to suit individual pupils, classes or schools. The activity sheets will be most effective when used to follow up a group or whole-class discussion.

Photocopiable activities

CHALLENGES

These photocopiable task cards offer creative challenges to individual pupils, pairs or groups. They can be given at any time and in any sequence. In order to complete these tasks pupils need to be able to follow the instructions, independent of the teacher.

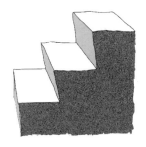

HOW TO USE THIS BOOK

QUICK STARTS

Quick starts contains a variety of short activities that can be used at any time during the day. They offer suggestions for relationship games, building positive routines, team co-operation, and recognising and rewarding good behaviour. These activities are intended to encourage the children to reflect on individual and general class behaviour.

Example

Icy poles (page 13) is ideal for encouraging pupils to work cooperatively together, in order to gain a reward.

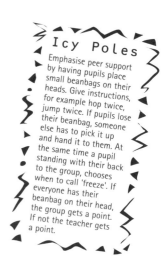

Icy Poles

Emphasise peer support by having pupils place small beanbags on their heads. Give instructions, for example hop twice, jump twice. If pupils lose their beanbag, someone else has to pick it up and hand it to them. At the same time a pupil standing with their back to the group, chooses when to call 'freeze'. If everyone has their beanbag on their head, the group gets a point. If not the teacher gets a point.

ACTIVITY BANK

These photocopiable activities can be used by individuals, groups or the whole class. They could provide the focus for a whole lesson and are important in promoting valuable discussion. The activities in themselves will not achieve the objectives, but they will make the children start to think about their behaviour and its effect on others. Some of the activities will touch on personal issues and this should be taken into consideration when introducing activities and discussing outcomes.

Example

When I feel angry (page 19) offers the pupils different strategies to help them deal with anger.

CHALLENGES

These activities are perfect for use in independent learning sessions where the focus is social interaction. They provide more practical activities for reinforcing behaviour management strategies previously covered in this book.

Example

Sock puppets (page 46) gives the pupils the opportunity to try out different strategies they could use to deal with angry feelings.

TASK CARD 1 — **Sock puppets**

What you need:
- old pair of socks
- four buttons for two pairs of eyes
- glue
- wool or cottonwool
- felt-tip pens
- scissors
- partner

What to do:
1. With a partner, plan a story which can be acted out with puppets.
2. Your story should include two people who get into a fight or have a disagreement.
3. Give the people in your story good ways to handle the disagreement or fight.
4. Each partner can make one sock puppet for the story. Glue two buttons as eyes onto the foot of each sock.
5. Attach wool or cotton wool as hair for your puppet.
6. Draw a nose and mouth on the 'face' of your puppet.
7. Act out the story.

TEACHERS' FILE

ABOUT BEHAVIOUR MANAGEMENT

Why do pupils misbehave?

- They feel as though they don't belong and so act out by misbehaving or getting into fights and arguments.
- They do not feel any sense of personal success at school.
- They do not have the personal skills to manage their behaviour and feelings.
- They feel disempowered because of negative feedback, either from peers or teachers, and express their anger through aggression or rule breaking.

There are also many reasons why groups of pupils misbehave, such as:

- What they are learning appears irrelevant, uninteresting or is taught in an unengaging fashion.
- There is a competitive and negative classroom climate.
- Pupils do not know each other well and have not developed positive relationships with each other.
- Expectations about how they should behave have not been made clear.
- Pupils do not have opportunities to learn to behave responsibly through decision making or undertaking important tasks.

'On-the-spot' management

It is important to deal with negative behaviour quickly and effectively. Apply appropriate and graduated consequences and where possible let the punishment 'fit the crime'.

Prevention

Build relationships and trust Relationship building helps to develop a positive and supportive classroom climate. Use activities and games to help pupils get to know and like each other.

Create a good relationship between yourself and your pupils Start with an expression of warmth and encouragement, focusing on their strengths rather than their weaknesses. Find something special about each pupil which you can talk to them about. Showing an interest in pupils will help to create a good working relationship.

Teach social skills Becoming more socially skilful enhances pupils' relationships with each other and creates a positive culture. You can teach pupils specific social skills, such as sharing, cooperating, resolving conflict, being positive, showing empathy, and maintaining friendships.

Teach personal skills You can also teach pupils personal skills which contribute to cooperation and self-discipline, such as anger management, understanding and handling feelings, being independent, and setting and achieving goals.

Establish a strong anti-bullying program Establish within the school that all forms of bullying are unacceptable. This may take a while but it is essential for creating the kind of safe, supportive and accepting environment which underpins good behaviour management.

Establish reward programs for appropriate behaviour Use strategies, games and activities which encourage good behaviour, such as finishing work, paying attention, not disrupting others and cooperating in groups. Set up rewards systems which are not expensive, do not attract envy from classmates, and are relevant to what is happening in the classroom (where possible).

Behavioural support

Some pupils find it more difficult than others to change their behaviour. For these pupils you may need to provide ongoing support, such as:

- An individual support plan which identifies what behavioural support will be offered, how and by whom.
- Peers to support them in changing their behaviour, e.g. a circle of friends.
- An individual behaviour contract between pupil and teacher with follow up rewards.
- Re-teaching of some specific skills in small groups.

CLASSROOM ORGANISATION

Build classroom relationships

Set aside some time every day in the first few weeks of term to start building a positive, supportive classroom environment. Use activities which help pupils get to know more about each other, using random groupings to enable each pupil to work at some point with every other classmate. Have pupils play educational games where they can have fun together and develop positive relationships so they feel safe to speak openly to each other. Give pupils many opportunities to make class decisions, give you feedback, and to negotiate.

Directly teach social skills, such as sharing and taking turns, listening well, being positive, negotiation, conflict management and respectful disagreeing. Use the four-step method when teaching social skills:
• discuss the skill
• outline the steps of how to gain the skill
• have pupils practise the skill using drama
• have pupils use the skill in a real activity, and give feedback.
Try to use cooperative learning at least once a day. It will not only improve the quality of learning for your pupils, but will also allow them opportunities to practise social skills and build relationships with each other.

Rights, responsibilities, relationships

Effective discipline is based on rights, responsibilities and relationships.
Pupils have the right to:
• the freedom to be themselves.
• the protection of both themselves and the things they own.
• the ability to concentrate on and enjoy their work without serious interruption.
• classroom surroundings which allow them to learn.
• a healthy and safe environment.

When a pupil violates one of these rights, you can ask 'Is what you're doing right or wrong?' Then extend this into a discussion about how their negative behaviour has affected the other pupils.

Use buddy systems

Cross-age buddy systems are an integral part of good behaviour management. For the older buddy, there are gains in maturity, empathic thinking, responsibility and social skills. Older pupils are less likely to give younger pupils a hard time when there are buddy systems in place, and more likely to act in a mature manner around their buddies. For the younger buddy there is the obvious benefit of a greater sense of safety, as well as feeling connected to an older pupil. The younger buddy also has the opportunity to see good social skills modelled.

Catch 'em being good

Establish effective reward systems which encourage good behaviour. Set up ways of giving whole class rewards when, as a group, they behave well. When necessary, negotiate individual contracts with specific pupils who are having more trouble than the others getting it right. With individual pupils you can either use individual rewards, or group rewards which they can earn and donate to the whole class (for example, group games).

CLASSROOM ORGANISATION

Classroom contracts

The most useful classroom contract is one that is negotiated between teacher and pupils and is relevant to their particular classroom climate. It should be introduced within the first week of term so that pupils are quickly aware of the behaviour expectations set. Page 42 features a classroom contract that will establish a commitment to positive behaviour.

Problem-solving mat

Teach the skills of conflict management. Make a 'Problem-solving mat' where pupils can be sent, or chose to go to sort out their conflict management issues. Tell pupils if they can't resolve things, you will mediate. Individual pupils could also use this mat as a place for 'time out' or for calming down.

Effective teaching

Effective teachers have fewer problems with behaviour management. Use engaging teaching strategies which are active and give pupils opportunities to socialise with each other in structured ways. Generate high curiosity by using many activities based around critical and creative thinking. Have fun with your pupils and express encouragement towards them. Be fair and consistent in the way you apply rules and deal with disputes, treating each individual pupil with respect. Share parts of yourself with your pupils and make what you teach relevant to pupils' lives.

Circle time

It is important to set aside some time each week where issues such as behaviour can be addressed as a whole class. It is an ideal time to allow pupils to discuss and explore their thoughts and feelings on a wide range of issues and events. Three simple rules should be established so that all pupils know:

- they must wait their turn before talking
- they must listen carefully to others
- they should show their interest by looking at the speaker.

Independence and cooperation

Explain to pupils that you expect them to think for themselves ('be their own boss'), and be helpful and work with you and other pupils in the classroom.

Teach cooperation and respect through discussion, and using the activities in this book. Try to use these terms when talking to pupils about their behaviour.

Refer to these behaviour styles when reprimanding pupils. For example, 'We try to be helpful in our classroom. How can you be more helpful?'; or by giving them positive feedback, 'Thank you for working well with the others. It made our class much better.'

A chance to shine

Give pupils the opportunity to take on responsible jobs at school, which will allow them to show others that they can organise, cooperate, lead and act confidently and gives them a sense of belonging. Use a range of teaching strategies that reflect different styles of learning, i.e. visual, auditory or kinaesthetic. Keep a record of your observations of pupils' relative strengths. On page 29 you will find a checklist called 'What are you best at?' for pupils to complete.

ICT TiPS

Computer time as a reward

Make computer time with a friend of their choice a reward for different behaviours, such as completion of work, improved behaviour for periods of time, or no hassles at playtime or lunchtime. Put a limit on the amount of time which can be earned as reward time, or make the amount of time earned reflect the degree of behavioural improvement. Alternatively have a reward menu on the computer so that individual pupils can browse the menu and select which reward they would like to earn. They can then set up their behaviour contract with the teacher using their ICT skills. Here are some ideas for rewards:

- helping out in a younger class for a session
- listening to music with headphones
- selecting a game to play with a group
- choosing an art and craft activity such as model making.

Partner computer games

Working on the computer is a useful context for teaching thoughtfulness and good manners. Arrange for pairs of pupils to play computer games together when feasible. Before they start, ask them to repeat for you the social skills required for working with partners. These are social skills such as:

- sharing and taking turns
- playing fairly and by the rules
- being a good winner and being a good loser
- paying attention to the game rather than being distracted
- having your go reasonably quickly rather than stalling.

Email feedback

Set up contact between a pupil and another significant adult in the school, whereby the pupil emails the adult (possibly another teacher or the deputy headteacher) when they have had periods of good behaviour or achieved goals. This tactic can also be used with parents if there is email at home.

Computer tutors

Even at an early age some pupils show an ability to quickly learn computer skills, especially if they have access to a computer at home. Put together a 'Computer Advisory Committee' of pupils who have knowledge and skills in specific areas of technology. This committee can be called on to teach others in the class a specific skill, assist the teacher, or be 'loaned' to another class as advisers. Similarly establish a 'Graphics Committee' of pupils who can easily produce computer graphics for posters, contracts, or certificates.

ASSESSMENT

Behaviour issues can be assessed by observing a pupil or group of pupils over time. Keeping a set of observations or record of events will enable you to compile an overall picture of behaviour patterns.

Observations
During observations of pupils ask yourself a number of questions that will provide useful information.

- What happens before he/she misbehaves?
- Does the behaviour occur in a particular place?
- Is there a certain pupil usually present?
- What are the specific behaviours that concern you?
- What positive reaction is the misbehaviour attracting, if any?

Encourage pupils to assess their own behaviour. This could involve a regular meeting between pupil and teacher, keeping a daily comment book or using some of the self evaluating worksheets in the activity bank.

PARENTAL INVOLVEMENT

It is important that pupil, teacher and parents work together when addressing behavioural issues. Parents need to be supportive of the school's approach to dealing with these problems. Good communication within this triangle is vital. Don't forget parents also need to hear about the improvements and achievements their child makes.

Encouraging news
Pupils get a real buzz when you tell their parents good things about them. Tell parents about improvements in behaviour or attitude using suggestions in the activity bank. Be as specific as possible (for example, 'Emma has

now developed a good relationship with two other girls in the class'). Make sure that certificates earned by pupils go home to their parents, and compile a list of certificates earned by each pupil.

The 'back of the door trick'
Send home a sheet with information about a skill you are working on, and ask parents to put a copy of the sheet somewhere where their child will see it. The back of the toilet door is a good place or under a fridge magnet.

Classroom photographic records
Take photographs of the life of the classroom and have pupils write descriptions. Let pupils take them home to show their parents. Make these available for parent-teacher interviews.

QUICK STARTS

Who's next?

Help pupils to get to know each other by arranging the class in a seated circle. Ask the first pupil to stand up and walk towards the second pupil in the circle, while saying that pupil's name. Ask the second pupil to start walking towards the third pupil while saying that pupil's name, before the first pupil gets to where the second pupil was standing. The task for the class as a whole is for everyone to be successfully named in this way with no-one going 'out'.

Name game

Play a relationship building game by helping pupils get to know something about each other. The first pupil says, 'My name is Jackie and I don't like pizza'. The next pupil says, 'She's Jackie who doesn't like pizza. I'm John and I play hockey'. It's similar to the game 'I went shopping' with the last pupil having to remember the details of every group member. Ask each pupil to say something about themselves which they think no-one else will say.

Practising routines

Practise routines in a fun way so that pupils 'overlearn' the most important ones, for example getting out materials, and moving from room to room or from activity to activity. Say 'We are going to practise getting ready to work. Let's see how quickly we can all get out our pens and be ready to write'. Then say 'That wasn't bad, let's see if we can do it within one minute next time.'

Spell it out

Take some time at the beginning of each year to make pupils familiar with your expectations regarding correct procedures for routines such as entering and leaving the room, using classroom materials or sharpening pencils. Go through the three or four steps for each routine many times. Remind pupils again just before the routine is used, for example 'What are our three rules for leaving a room thoughtfully?'

Music! Music! Music!

Use music to signal instructions to pupils. Play a 'boppy' song which is about 90 seconds long and let pupils know that they have to be lined up for class by the end of the song. You can also use this to signal '90 seconds to go before we go out to lunch, please pack up now!' Make sure the song is a popular one.

Chinese whispers

Remind pupils that they should listen more than they speak by referring to the wise owl who, 'the more he heard, the less he spoke; the less he spoke, the more he heard'. (Listening ability is important in developing social skills.) Pupils can draw a listening owl. Practise with 'Chinese Whispers' where each pupil repeats what they have been told by the person next to them. The message gets distorted, demonstrating how easy it is to listen incorrectly!

There and back

Pair pupils up with someone they don't know very well. Label them 'A' and 'B'. Give them a conversational topic such as 'my perfect meal'. Nominate a 'finish line'. On the way to the 'finish line' only person A person talks. On the way back, only person B talks. This offers a chance to practise the social skills of listening and being interesting.

Hands up for silence!

Discuss how most people don't like raised voices. Explain that you will raise your hand when you want them to stop work, quieten down and listen to you. As soon as each pupil sees the raised hand signal, they should stop talking and raise their hand too. The ripple effect will have the class silent very quickly. It takes a little time to practise this however, so be patient.

Icy poles

Emphasise peer support by having pupils place small beanbags on their heads. Give instructions, for example hop twice, jump twice. If pupils lose their beanbag, someone else has to pick it up and hand it to them. At the same time a pupil standing with their back to the group, chooses when to call 'freeze'. If everyone has their beanbag on their head, the group gets a point. If not the teacher gets a point.

Broken record

Use the 'broken record' strategy when a pupil does not obey a direction. State what you want them to do in a sentence which starts 'I want you to...'. If there is no response, repeat the instruction. If the pupil argues, ignore what they said and then repeat the direction a third time. If there is still no action from the pupil, add a statement of consequence.

Smiley cards

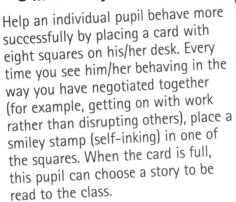

Help an individual pupil behave more successfully by placing a card with eight squares on his/her desk. Every time you see him/her behaving in the way you have negotiated together (for example, getting on with work rather than disrupting others), place a smiley stamp (self-inking) in one of the squares. When the card is full, this pupil can choose a story to be read to the class.

Lucky dip rewards

Place a number of group treat vouchers (for example, time with the radio on, extra playtime) in a lucky dip bag. Agree with pupils on the specific behaviours which are being assessed. Keep a star chart recording how often the class uses that behaviour, for example cooperates or works quietly. When the class has earned the specified number of stars, one pupil draws a reward voucher for the whole class.

Smiley ball

You will need a light ball with a smiley face for this game. Pupils sit in a circle and you begin the game by rolling the smiley ball to a pupil, saying that child's name. They in turn roll the ball to another pupil, and say that pupil's name, and the game continues in this way.

The smiley ball can also be used for pupils to say something they like about the person to whom they roll the ball.

'Do not disturb' table

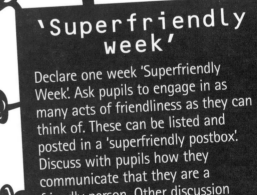

Set aside a table in the classroom which faces away from the rest of the class and preferably has a small screen along one side to reduce distractions. Pupils who are disrupting others or not getting on with their work can be asked to go and work for ten minutes on the 'Do Not Disturb' table. Put a timer on the desk and when it goes off they can return to their own table and resume work.

'Superfriendly week'

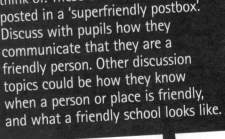

Declare one week 'Superfriendly Week'. Ask pupils to engage in as many acts of friendliness as they can think of. These can be listed and posted in a 'superfriendly postbox'. Discuss with pupils how they communicate that they are a friendly person. Other discussion topics could be how they know when a person or place is friendly, and what a friendly school looks like.

Special cupboard

Keep one cupboard as the classroom's 'special cupboard'. Keep your card games, board games, jigsaws, puzzles and toys here which are used only for special rewards. Use the contents of this cupboard as rewards for pupils with whom you have negotiated contracts regarding work and behaviour improvements. You can allow pupils rewards such as playing for twenty minutes with a friend, using any equipment of choice from the 'special cupboard'. Remember, it is also important to reward the children who are continuously well-behaved.

Caring trees

Put a small branch of a tree (no leaves) into a pot of sand. Have pupils make paper leaves and flowers which will be attached to the branch. Explain that every time someone in the class tells you about someone else's behaviour which was supportive, caring, generous or friendly, you will write that person's name and what they did on a leaf or flower, and hang it on the caring tree.

Movers and shakers

Involve pupils in a 'movers and shakers' discussion—useful for when pupils have been sitting still for too long and are losing concentration or becoming disruptive. Standing up, they answer 'yes' to your questions by doing movements. For example 'If you like spaghetti, make a helicopter movement with your arms' or 'If you have been to the zoo, make a trunk movement like an elephant.' You could choose questions which reflect what you are teaching.

I'm not surprised!

Check with teachers who were on playground duty and if there were no problems with your pupils, say to your class 'No problems at playtime with any one here. I'm not surprised'. One pupil selects a marble and drops it into the 'Good behaviour jar'. When there are thirty of them, play a favourite class game.

Chances

Draw six circles on the board and put a '5' inside each (standing for 5 minutes). Tell pupils that you expect everyone to be getting on with their work and that any time you see someone being unhelpful or not working, you will cross off one circle. The number of circles that are left towards the end of the day will represent how many minutes of free time pupils will get.

CIRCLE TIME QUICK STARTS

Circle time has become an important part of the Key Stage 1 timetable. It is flexible enough to be used in most subject areas and can naturally link areas of the curriculum. It is particularly appropriate for discussions raised within the PSHE and Citizenship Framework.

Say hello

It is important that a class of children are given opportunities to get to know each other. Sitting in a circle ensures everybody can see all the pupils in their class. A simple beginning to circle time is to pass around a 'Hello' accompanied by a handshake. Repeat the exercise adding more information each time. For example, 'Hello, my name is Andrew.' Next time you might say, 'Hello, my name is Andrew and I have got a pet dog called Bobby.'

Circle time etiquette

Three simple rules should be followed when carrying out a circle time session:
• Only talk when it is your turn.
• Listen carefully to the child who is talking.
• Look towards the child that is talking.

To help the children learn these rules, choose a circle time object such as a teddy bear. Tell the children they can only talk when they have the teddy bear sitting on their lap. This will encourage them to focus on the pupil with the chosen object. The object used at circle time can be changed for each session.

Discussing feelings

Circle time is a useful tool for dealing with current issues or events that are upsetting children in the class. Place key words such as sad, worried, unhappy or lonely in the middle of the circle and ask children to discuss when or what makes them feel like this. This can be particularly good for following events that have happened in the playground, for example a child being excluded by their group of friends. When discussions of this nature are taking place it is important to use the 'no names' rule. The 'no names' rule means that pupils are not allowed to name other children in the school who have caused these feelings.

Magic stone

Circle time sessions can be used to encourage children's creativity and imagination. Give them an interesting object like a large smooth pebble and tell them it is magical. Ask a child to rub the magic stone and describe what they imagine would happen next!

Character hats

Put a selection of hats in the middle of the circle and give the pupils a situation. The children can chose the character they wish to play, and may use a hat or any other props they feel are in role. The situation can then be acted out. You can extend this activity by asking for pupils who feel they can act out the same characters in a different way.

ACTIVITY BANK

Making up

If you have had a fight with someone, fill in this sheet to help you work out how to sort it out.

I want _____

_____

I feel _____

_____

I feel like this because _____

_____

I think they feel _____

_____

I think they want _____

_____

Two things we could do to solve our problem:

1. _____

2. _____

Teaches the skills of conflict management.

NAME

When I feel angry

Below each box is a way to deal with feeling angry. If you have used any of these, write about what you did in the box. Or, if you think you need to get better at any of these things, draw a picture in the box showing what you might do next time you get angry.

I think about what could be my fault.	I talk to someone about my angry feelings.	I do something else to take my mind off it.

I try hard to see their side of it.	I do some exercise and then I feel better.

Teaches anger management skills.

Can you do it?

This is a contract between

_____ and _____
(Teacher's name)   (Pupil's name)

I, _____ (pupil) agree that I will

_____

_____

_____

_____

I will do this by _____ (date).

Pupil's signature: _____   Date: _____

I, _____ (teacher) agree that if
_____ (pupil) follows what has
been agreed in this contract, then I will provide

_____

_____

_____

_____

Teacher's signature: _____   Date: _____

Individual behaviour contracts.

Giant

Imagine that a giant has enrolled in your class. How do you think the giant would feel?

_____

_____

_____

How could you and your classmates help the giant settle in?

_____

_____

What changes could be made in the classroom to make things easier for the giant?

_____

_____

On the back of this sheet draw yourself sitting next to the giant.

Teaches social skills.

Which one is telling tales?

- **Telling tales** is just trying to get someone into trouble and not trying to solve the problem yourself.
- **Asking for support** is asking a teacher to help you solve a problem that you haven't been able to solve by yourself.
- **Acting responsibly** is letting a teacher or other adult know when something bad is happening to you or someone else in your class.

Look at the pictures below and then decide whether the person is telling tales, asking for support or acting responsibly. Circle the words which describe what is happening.

Telling tales
Asking for support
Acting responsibly

Telling tales   Asking for support   Acting responsibly

Telling tales   Asking for support   Acting responsibly

Teaches personal skills.

Being noticed

Here are some good ways and some bad ways to be noticed by other people in the class. Colour the good ways in blue and the bad ways in yellow.

Showing off

Starting up a game

Telling a funny story

Making a nasty joke about someone

Helping another person

Breaking a rule

Being good at something

Refusing to go out in a game

Being kind to someone

Teaches personal skills.

We are detectives

Try to find a different person in your class for each of the descriptions below.

 Someone taller than I am is _____

 Someone smaller than I am is _____

 Someone with curly hair is _____

 Someone with straight hair is _____

 Someone who sits near me is _____

 Someone who likes dogs is _____

 Someone who likes cats is _____

Builds relationships/getting to know others.

Guess who is different

Cut out each of the labels below and fold along the dotted line. On the outside of the label write something about yourself which makes you different to everyone else in the class. On the inside of the label write the answer—YOUR NAME! Add your labels to a board displaying other labels, and take turns to guess who is different.

Name:

Name:

Name:

Name:

Builds relationships/getting to know others.

Kicking goals

Cut out the footballs. Write your name and a goal (something you are working towards) on each football. You can also colour in each of your footballs. When you have achieved your goal, or a step towards your goal, attach a football between the goalposts on page 27.

Fosters goal setting and develops a sense of personal success.

I reached my goal!

Fosters goal setting and develops a sense of personal success.

Success chains

Each time you achieve a goal or step write it down on one of the rectangular strips.

When all the strips are filled in, colour each strip a different colour and cut them out. Glue the ends of each strip together to make a circle (so you can still see your name and goal) and then link the circles together to make a chain.

Hang the chain from your chair or display on a wall.

Name: Goal achieved:
Name: Goal achieved:
Name: Goal achieved:
Name: Goal achieved:
Name: Goal achieved:
Name: Goal achieved:

Fosters goal setting and develops a sense of personal success.

What are you best at?

Colour each box, using the colours in the key. Only six boxes can be coloured red.

Key			
Red means I am really really good at this.	Blue means I am very good at this.	Green means I am pretty good at this.	Yellow means I am just okay at this.

Writing stories (Word)	 Doing maths (Logic and maths)	Playing sport (Body)	 Playing a musical instrument (Music)
 Growing things (Science)	 Dancing (Body)	Knowing how I feel (Self)	 Helping people (People)
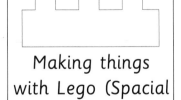 Making things with Lego (Spacial awareness)	 Computers (Logic and maths)	 Reading (Word)	Making friends easily (People)
 Singing well (Music)	 Understanding animals (Science)	 Drawing (Spacial awareness)	Deciding what I want and doing it (Self)

Encourages children to recognise their own strengths.

Communities and teams

What would happen if these groups of people did not cooperate with each other?

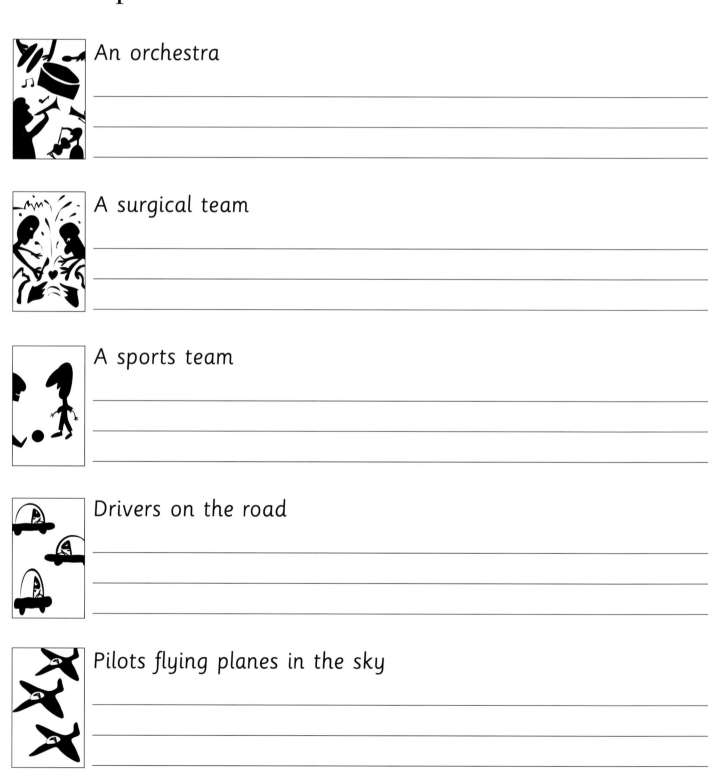

An orchestra

A surgical team

A sports team

Drivers on the road

Pilots flying planes in the sky

Fosters concept of cooperation.

Being independent

Draw yourself when you have finished your work and have no other work to do. What would you choose to do now?

I am being independent and choosing to

Draw yourself when you have no one to play with in the playground. What would you choose to do now?

I am being independent and choosing to

Expects and encourages independence and cooperation.

Our circle time

Colour in the face to show how well you followed our class's circle time rules.
A happy face means you followed the rules; a sad face means you need to try harder in circle time.

I raised my hand if I wanted to say something and waited until the teacher said it was my turn.

I did not laugh at what others said.

I tried to say something even when I felt shy.

I listened to what others had to say.

Expects and encourages independence and cooperation.

Animal grouping

Photocopy the set of eight cards three times (this allows for 24 pupils). Paste on cardboard, cut out and mix cards in a container. Have pupils pick a card each, and imitate the noise the animal on their card makes. The aim is for them to find the other two pupils making a similar noise. (Alternatively you could ask pupils to do animal actions.)

Develops cooperation.

Group work reflections

After a group work activity ask each pupil to complete the following.

Your name: _____

The people in our group were:

_____

_____

_____

The activity which we did was:

_____

_____

_____

Colour in the face which shows how well you worked together.

We worked very well together.   We worked quite well together.   We worked okay together.   We didn't work well together.

What helped your group work well together?

_____

_____

_____

What stopped your group from cooperating with each other?

_____

_____

_____

Develops cooperation.

Rules!

1. Write down two rules you have at home.

_____

_____

_____

2. What is a rule we have in our community?

_____

_____

_____

3. What happens to people who break the rules in our community?

_____

_____

_____

4. Do you think rules are good things to have? Why or why not?

_____

_____

_____

_____

Teaches social and moral responsibility.

Classroom contract quiz

1. What is our classroom rule about _____?

_____

_____

_____

2. What is our classroom rule about _____?

_____

_____

_____

3. What is our classroom rule about _____?

_____

_____

_____

4. What is our classroom rule about _____?

_____

_____

_____

5. What is our classroom rule about _____?

_____

_____

_____

Teaches social and moral responsibility.

How are we doing?

Interview pupils individually, or in pairs, and ask them the following questions to find out how things are going.

Pupil(s):	Date:

- Do people in this class share and take turns when you work with them?

  _____

  _____

- Do you have many friends in this class?

  _____

  _____

- Is this class a nice place to be for you?

  _____

  _____

- Do you usually have someone to play with at playtime and lunchtime?

  _____

  _____

- Do you ever feel unhappy about playing a game?

  _____

  _____

- Do you feel lonely or left out a lot?

  _____

  _____

- Do you look forward to coming to school each day?

  _____

  _____

- Why?

  _____

  _____

Assesses pupils.

Classroom circles

One circle will be coloured in by me whenever the skill of
_____ (behaviour) is reported or observed being
used by a member of our class. You need _____ circles to earn
the reward _____.

Establishes rewards systems.

Good News!

has shown improvement in the following ways:

_____

_____

_____

_____

_____

_____

_____

_____

Teacher's signature:

_____

Date:

_____

Develops classroom values and social skills.

Friendliness Certificate

This friendliness certificate is awarded to

_____

for the friendliness which they showed when they

_____

_____

_____

Teacher's signature   Date

_____   _____

Kindness Certificate

This kindness certificate is awarded to

_____

for the kindness which they showed when they

_____

_____

_____

Teacher's signature   Date

_____   _____

Develops classroom values and social skills.

Name: _____

List of certificates earned

Certificate title	Date awarded	Teacher's signature

Develops classroom values and social skills.

Our classroom contract

Contract between Class _____ and the
teacher _____

All members of Class _____ agree that:
- We will be friendly and thoughtful to each other.
- We will never say 'you cannot play with us'.
- We will cooperate with each other.
- We will look after our equipment or lose the
  chance to use it.
- We will remember to work quietly, not disturbing
  the work of others.
- We will always be careful not to hurt each other
  or each other's feelings.

Teacher's signature: _____ Date: _____

Pupils' signatures:

Encourages social and moral responsibility.

What can you tell me about your child?

Obviously, there are interesting things about your child which I and their fellow classmates might not know. Could you please fill in the following details about your child's interests and achievements and return it to me by

_____

Thank you.

Teacher's signature _____

Name:

Interests: _____
_____
_____

Strengths: _____
_____
_____

Achievements: _____
_____
_____

Skills: _____
_____
_____

Positive character traits: _____
_____
_____

Anything else you would like to mention: _____
_____
_____

CHALLENGES

Sock puppets

What you need:

- old pair of socks
- four buttons for two pairs of eyes
- glue
- wool or cotton wool
- felt-tip pens
- scissors
- a partner

What to do:

1. With a partner, plan a story which can be acted out with puppets.
2. Your story should include two people who get into a fight or have a disagreement.
3. Give the people in your story good ways to handle the disagreement or fight.
4. Each partner can make one sock puppet for the story. Glue two buttons as eyes onto the foot of each sock.
5. Attach wool or cotton wool as hair for your puppet.
6. Draw a nose and mouth on the 'face' of your puppet.
7. Act out the story.

Lucky dip draw

What you need:

- thin cardboard or paper
- scissors
- felt-tip pens, crayons, pencils

What to do:

1. Decide what reward you would like to put on your lucky dip voucher. It could be playing a game with a friend, choosing a story for the class, or a wild card voucher (the person who gets this voucher can decide what their reward will be).
2. Cut out cardboard or paper into any shape you like.
3. Write the reward on your voucher.
4. Decorate the voucher with felt-tip pens, crayons, pencils.
5. Post the voucher into the lucky dip box. (You may need to make and design the lucky dip box as well!)

Feedback booklets

What you need:

- five pieces of thin cardboard or paper
- scissors
- felt-tip pens, crayons, pencils

What to do:

1. On the first piece of cardboard or paper draw a very happy face with a speech bubble saying 'I felt confident about doing this.' This is the first page of your booklet.
2. On the second piece draw a happy face saying 'I felt okay about doing this.'
3. On the third piece draw a face (with a straight line for a mouth) saying 'This was a bit hard for me.'
4. On the fourth piece draw a worried face saying 'I didn't enjoy this.'
5. On the fifth piece draw a very worried face saying 'This made me feel unhappy.'
6. Staple the five pieces together (in order) to make your feedback booklet.
7. Use your booklet to show your teacher at the end of an activity how you felt about doing it.

'People I know' mobile

What you need:

- coat hanger
- light cardboard
- scissors
- string to hang your pictures on the coat hanger
- felt-tip pens, crayons, pencils

What to do:

1. Cut up your cardboard into five different shapes.
2. Choose five people in your class who you don't know very well.
3. Find out one thing about each of them. (You could ask about their pets, family, favourite games or their holidays.)
4. Listen carefully to their answers.
5. Write the person's name and the thing you found out about them on one of your shapes.
6. Repeat Step 5 for the other people.
7. Make a hole in the top of each of your five shapes.
8. Thread string through the holes.
9. Hang the five cards from the coat hanger by tying the string.
10. Display your mobile in the classroom.

Sharks and owls

What you need:

- cardboard

- scissors

- felt-tip pens, crayons, pencils

- sticky tape (clear tape is best)

What to do:

1. Draw your own shark and owl. (Sharks hurt people to get what they want. Owls are smarter and try to solve problems.)

2. Colour the shark yellow. Write NO and put a big cross (X) on it.

3. Cut it out and stick it on a display area in your classroom.

4. Colour the owl blue, write YES and put a big tick on it.

5. Cut it out and write your name on it.

6. Display your owl where everyone can see.

TASK CARD 6

My favourite things

What you need:

- a picture from a magazine of something you like very much (for example, an animal, a flower, a scene, a vehicle).

- scissors

- white cardboard

- glue

- felt-tip pen

What to do:

1. Cut out your picture.

2. Paste it onto the white cardboard.

3. Cut around your picture on the cardboard.

4. Write your name on the back of your picture.

5. Give the picture to your teacher. When your teacher wants to tell you that you are making a great effort, they will put your picture on your desk to let you know.

 **TASK CARD 7**

Unkind thumb

What you need:

- light-coloured paper
- cardboard
- pen
- scissors
- glue
- red felt-tip pen

What to do:

1. Draw around your hand on the white paper, but make your thumb a lot bigger than the rest of your hand.

2. Cut it out and glue it onto cardboard.

3. Cut around the hand on the cardboard.

4. Colour the thumb with the red felt tip pen.

5. Whenever you think someone says or does something which is unkind, place your unkind thumb on the teacher's desk.

 **TASK CARD 8**

Thank you card

What you need:

- white cardboard
- scissors
- felt-tip pens, crayons, pencils

What to do:

1. Cut out ten rectangular shapes about 20 cm by 10 cm.

2. Fold in half to form a card.

3. In big letters on the front of each card write 'Thank you!'

4. Decorate the front as well.

5. Inside the card write a message and sign your name.

6. Put one of your thank you cards on the desk of anyone who has given you help or been friendly, and tell them why you have given it to them.